WITHDRAWN

Chaco Canyon

digging
for the past

BRIAN FAGAN, General Editor

Chaco Canyon

R. Gwinn Vivian
and Margaret Anderson

OXFORD
UNIVERSITY PRESS

To Norm

OXFORD
UNIVERSITY PRESS

Oxford   New York

Auckland   Bangkok   Buenos Aires   Cape Town   Chennai   Dar es Salaam
Delhi   Hong Kong   Istanbul   Karachi   Kolkata   Kuala Lumpur   Madrid
Melbourne   Mexico City   Mumbai   Nairobi   São Paulo   Shanghai   Singapore
Taipei   Tokyo   Toronto   and an associated company in Berlin

Copyright © 2002 by Oxford University Press, Inc.
Published by Oxford University Press, Inc.
198 Madison Avenue, New York, New York   10016
www.oup.com

Design: Kingsley Parker   Layout: Karla Roberts

Library of Congress Cataloging-in-Publication Data

Vivian, R. Gwinn
Chaco Canyon / R. Gwinn Vivian & Margaret Anderson
p. cm. — (Digging for the past)
Includes bibliographical references and index.
ISBN 0-19-514280-2
1. Pueblo Indians--New Mexico--Chaco Canyon--Anquities--Juvenile lierature. 2. Cliff-
dwellings--New Mexico--Chaco Canyon--Juvenile literature. 3. Chaco Canyon (N.M.)--
Antiquities--Juvenile literature. 4. Chaco Culture National Historical Park (N.M.)--
Juvenile literature. [1. Pueblo Indians--Antiquities. 2. Indians of North America--New
Mexico--Antiquities. 3. Cliff dwellings--New Mexico--Chaco Canyon. 4 Chaco Canyon
(N.M.)--Antiquities.] I. Anderson, Margaret Jean, 1931– II. Title. III. Series.

E99.P9 V573 2002
978.9'2—dc21   2001054855

9 8 7 6 5 4 3 2 1

Printed in Hong Kong on acid-free paper.

Picture Credits: American Museum of Natural History: 12, 14; Thomas Clark: 16; Library
of Congress (LC-USZ62-094089): 27; Paul Logsdon: 8; Museum of New Mexico (neg.
44257): 13; National Park Service, Chaco Canyon National Historical Park: 1 (Alden
Hays), 2 (Robert Greenlee), 3 (Dave Six), 5 (Dave Six), 9, 10, 15, 20 (Dave Six), 21, 22,
26 (Paul Sneed), 29, 30, 31 (Alden Hays), 32 (Richard Meleski), 33 (Dave Six), 36
(Dave Six), 37, 38 (Dave Sifler), 39, 40 (Dabney Ford); Gary Tong: 6 (maps), 11, 25,
48; Gwinn Vivian: 4, 19, 23, 33, 34 (drawings), 35, 41, 42, 45.

Cover: Against the back-
drop of Pueblo Bonito,
two archaeologists gather
data about their site.
Frontispiece: Excavation of
a pithouse in Chaco
Canyon.

Contents

Where and When

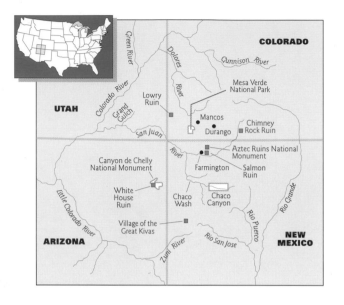

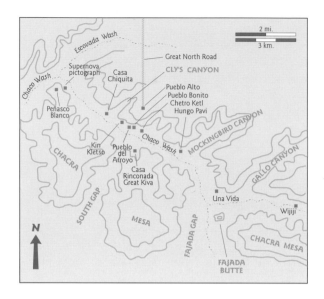

Archaeological History

1823

Mexican governor José Antonio Vizcarra records existence of Chacoan ruins

1849

U.S. Army Lt. James Simpson documents Chacoan ruins

1896

Richard Wetherill excavates Pueblo Bonito great house

1920

Edgar L. Hewett begins excavations at Chetro Ketl great house

1921

Neil Judd starts five-year excavation program in Chacoan ruins

1929

Edgar L. Hewett begins student archaeological field training at Chetro Ketl great house

1936

University of New Mexico opens field school in Chaco Canyon; work begins on small-house sites

1971

National Park Service and University of New Mexico establish Chaco Center for excavation and research

1997

National Park Service and University of Colorado begin to combine their data on Chacoan prehistory

Ancient History

Date	Phase	Event
1500 B.C.	Archaic Period	◄ Hunting and gathering peoples establish seasonal camps
A.D. 400	Archaic Period	◄ Simple farming begins
700		◄ Basket Maker peoples establish farm settlements, including large sites with great kivas
900	Early Bonito Phase	◄ Early pueblo peoples live in small farm settlements
		◄ Mesa Verde peoples move in
		◄ Three early great houses (Pueblo Bonito, Una Vida, Peñasco Blanco) built; many small-house sites occupied
1040	Classic Bonito Phase	◄ Great houses and great kivas built; water-control systems developed; roads laid out to connect canyon with great houses in San Juan Basin; small-house sites occupied
1100	Late Bonito Phase	◄ Last construction of great houses and small-house sites
1140		◄ Chacoan peoples abandon canyon and move south (Zuni area) and east (Rio Grande Valley)
1220		◄ Mesa Verde peoples reoccupy some great houses, including Pueblo Bonito, and build several new pueblos in canyon
1350		

1

The House with 800 Rooms

A north–south wall divides the courtyard in the middle of Pueblo Bonito's D-shape. Rooms and kivas cluster around the central, open space.

Long before state boundaries were drawn, American Indians lived on a high plateau in an area that is now known as the Four Corners, because it is the place where the corners of four states meet. Cliff dwellings and many-roomed buildings, known as pueblos, still dot the landscape. They are the work of an ancient civilization of people we call the Anasazi. Their huge deserted buildings in Chaco Canyon, New Mexico; Canyon de Chelly, Arizona; Grand Gulch, Utah; and Mesa Verde, Colorado, provide present-day visitors and archaeologists an exciting glimpse of the distant past.

Chaco Canyon is a remote and lonely place in northwest New Mexico that stretches for about 20 miles between high sandstone cliffs. The wind whips clouds of dry, sandy soil through the olive-green greasewood bushes scattered across the canyon floor and swirls around the ragged walls of the silent ruins of ancient buildings that once rang with shouting and laughter. A thousand years ago, people lived in the canyon in 11 "great houses," each one of them big enough to provide homes for an entire village. These long-ago people dug ditches to carry water to their fields of corn, beans, and squash. They constructed wide, straight roads to connect with the world outside the canyon. They built circular underground rooms called kivas, where they gathered to perform special rituals and ceremonies.

The sandstone cliffs that border the canyon have been carved by wind and water so that they look like giant heads watching over the ancient great houses. The houses all have names, such as Pueblo Bonito, Chetro Ketl, Peñasco Blanco, and Wijiji, that were given to them much later. In Spanish, Pueblo Bonito means Beautiful Town and Peñasco Blanco means White Rock Point. There is no English translaton for Wijiji or Chetro Ketl; these names were given to the houses by local Indians in the 19th century. We will never know what they were called by the people who built them. We do not really know who these people were, but through archaeology we are gradually forming a picture of their long-lost civilization.

For the last 100 years, archaeologists have been piecing together the story of life in Chaco Canyon. We now know when the ancient people who lived there started building the great houses and when they stopped. We know what they wore and what they ate. We know about their baskets, their pottery, and their tools. They fashioned turquoise into beads and pendants in their workshops. They traded with people as far away as the Pacific coast and Mexico.

At the same time, there is still a lot we do not know—and may never know. Why did they build these great houses in that desolate place? Why are most of the buildings clustered in that particular stretch of the 20-mile-long canyon? Why were they abandoned?

The towering slab of sandstone cliff known as Threatening Rock crashed down on Pueblo Bonito in January 1941, destroying about 65 rooms in the great house. Ancient Chacoans had built a wall below the rock and placed prayer offerings on the wall to protect their home—measures that appear to have worked for centuries.

What happened to the people? These unsolved mysteries are what make the ancient ruins so intriguing.

The first person to try to find answers to these questions was Richard Wetherill, a Quaker rancher and self-taught archaeologist. His passion for archaeology dated back to discovering the cliff dwellings in Mesa Verde in southwest Colorado. One cold December day in 1888, he and his brother-in-law were searching for stray cattle on Mesa Verde, a large flat-topped mountain close to the Wetherill ranch at Mancos, Colorado. While the two men rested their horses, they walked out to a windswept rock that overlooked a deep canyon. Directly across the canyon, through lightly falling snow, they saw dark, empty windows and doorways staring back at them from a maze of walls and tapering towers that had been built in a deep opening in the face of the cliff. Wetherill named the place Cliff Palace.

Wetherill was fascinated with the idea that unknown people had once lived in these high, vacant rooms. He returned again and again to Cliff Palace to look for clues about this lost civilization of cliff dwellers. He concluded that they must have lived there a very long time ago, because some of the artifacts he discovered were buried under several feet of wind-blown sand and dirt that had washed down from the surrounding cliffs. He found sandals that people had worn, pots they had made, and other artifacts from their daily lives. He also found human bones.

He set up a small museum of his finds at his ranch, which soon became a magnet for visitors with an interest in archaeology. Two of these visitors, Fred and Talbot Hyde, were wealthy young brothers who would later play a big part in the excavations in Chaco Canyon.

Richard Wetherill's interest in the Mesa Verde cliff dwellers and their artifacts took him to other areas in search of ancient ruins. One of these places was Grand Gulch, a winding, 50-mile-long canyon in Utah that was full of cliff dwellings and burial sites.

A Chacoan sandal woven from the long, tough leaves of the yucca plant. Chacoans also used yucca leaves as shoelaces, which they ran through loops along the edge of the sandal.

He soon realized that a succession of people had lived in the area. The earliest settlers had not made pottery and had no bows and arrows. Instead they used a dart or spear propelled by a throwing stick called an atlatl. They wove beautiful baskets from willow and the yucca plant, so Wetherill called them the Basket Makers. They made their baskets in many sizes. He found some that measured four or five feet across and had been used to cover burials. He noted that the skulls of the Basket Makers were not flattened on the back like those of people Wetherill called Cliff Dwellers. From this he guessed that the Basket Makers did not strap their babies to cradle boards—a practice that results in flattened head bones.

Late in 1895 the Palmers, a family of traveling musicians, visited the Wetherill ranch. They were an unusual family who were paying their way through the Southwest by giving concerts. Nineteen-year-old Marietta had a lovely singing voice. Her younger brother and sister played the flute and violin.

The Palmers had heard rumors about ancient ruins in Chaco Canyon and wanted to visit them. Wetherill offered to accompany them. During the month they camped in the canyon Wetherill was amazed by what they saw. He described the ruins in a letter to the Hyde brothers as "the greatest in New Mexico and almost unknown." Hoping the brothers would finance an expedition, he told them: "I was successful after a few days search in finding relics in quantity—the ruins there are enormous—there are 11 of the large Pueblos of houses containing from one hundred to 500 rooms each and numerous small ones. . . . A wagon can be driven to the Ruins in 5 or six days from our Ranch." His enthusiasm paid off. The Hyde Exploring Expedition spent the next five years excavating Pueblo Bonito, the biggest of the great houses.

Wetherill did not spend the entire month in Chaco Canyon exploring the ruins. He also found time to fall in love with Marietta. They were married in December of the following year and spent their honeymoon on an expedition to Grand Gulch.

An ancient hunter throws a spear with an atlatl, a board with a hook on its end to hold the weapon until he lets go.

Marietta's wandering childhood proved to be good preparation for the rough life in an archaeology camp. She took even the most unexpected situations in her stride. One night, Wetherill looked out from the shallow cave where they slept and saw that it was snowing. He struggled out of his bedroll, muttering something about being afraid that the mummies he had found might get wet. A short time later, he returned carrying two shriveled figures and asked his bride if she wanted them next to her head or her feet. She replied, "At the foot, Mr. Wetherill. At the foot of the bed."

Marietta usually called her husband Mr. Wetherill, which sounds strange to our ears but was common among many married couples at that time. He affectionately called her by the Navajo name Asthanne, which means Little Woman. After they moved to Chaco, Wetherill had a nickname, too, given him by his Navajo workers. They called him Anasazi, the name they used for the ancestors that fascinated him. Because the prehistoric people are related to Pueblo-dwelling people, such as the Hopis and the Zunis, and Anasazi is a Navajo word, the ancient ancestors are now usually referred to as Chacoans or Ancestral Puebloans.

The Wetherills moved to Chaco Canyon in the spring of 1897. It would be Marietta's home until after Richard's death in 1910. They had five children and lived in a small stone

Pueblo Bonito as it appeared in 1895, before Richard Wetherill began his excavations.

house built next to the west wall of
Pueblo Bonito. The roof was supported
by beams removed from Bonito during
excavation. Later, Wetherill was severely
criticized for doing this. Because the
modern approach is to disturb a site as
little as possible, no one would think of
"borrowing" timbers from a dig today,
but early archaeologists in the Southwest worked under tremendously difficult conditions. All their supplies—
tents, shovels, flour, sugar, sides of beef,
grain, and bales of hay—had to be
hauled in from Mancos, Colorado, by
horse-drawn wagons across 150 rough
miles. The climate was severe, with
scorching summers and frigid winters.
There were no trees for shade—or for roof beams.

*One of the Wetherill broth-
ers explores an early rock
shelter in southern Utah.*

George Pepper from the American Museum of Natural History
in New York City was the scientific director of the Hyde
Expedition. He and Wetherill worked together excavating the
rooms in Pueblo Bonito, measuring every feature and taking many
photographs. This was not a simple task. Cameras in those days
were big and clumsy and used glass plates instead of film. In all,
they excavated 190 rooms. The work was slow, but the rewards
were great. Any day, they might uncover hidden treasure. In one
room they dug up 114 jars, 22 bowls, and 21 jar covers. Another
room held the skeleton of a man who must have been important,
judging from the jewelry buried with him. Bands of turquoise
beads encircled his wrists and ankles. Around his neck and waist
were pendants made from 5,000 pieces of turquoise.

Everything of interest that the two men found was recorded
and crated up to send back to the American Museum of Natural
History. By the end of the first season, they had dug up enough

This cache of Chacoan pottery was just one layer of a rich deposit of jars and bowls that Richard Wetherill discovered in a room in Pueblo Bonito. The rare cylinder jars were probably used for special ceremonies.

artifacts to fill an entire freight car. All their finds had to be carried by horse or mule to the railroad station at Durango, Colorado.

Although the expedition was very successful, not everyone was happy. Edgar Hewett, president of New Mexico Normal University, did not like the idea that artifacts from New Mexico were being shipped to a museum in the East. A rumor went around that Wetherill was getting rich by selling artifacts; that was not true. Critics also brought up the matter of the roof beams. Because of these controversies, the Hyde brothers closed down the work at Pueblo Bonito. But there was a positive result, too. The complaints led Congress to pass the Antiquities Act of 1906 to preserve the nation's ancient ruins. The following year, Chaco Canyon became a National Monument. Seventy-three years later, in 1980, the monument area was enlarged to take in related ancient communities, and Chaco Canyon became part of the Chaco Culture National Historical Park.

The great houses of Chaco Canyon lay essentially undisturbed until 1921, when the National Geographic Society sent out an expedition under the leadership of Neil Judd, who was a curator of the National Museum of Natural History at the Smithsonian Institution in Washington, D.C. During the seasons Judd worked at Chaco, he brought with him a crew of anywhere from three to seven people (always including a cook). He hired local Navajos to help with the digging and also brought in a crew of Zuni Indians.

Judd knew that a good way to date a civilization in the Southwest was by studying its pottery. Designs painted on the pots changed over time. Pottery could also be used to trace waves of incoming people. But first Judd needed to chart all the design

changes. He decid-
ed to begin by
examining pottery
from Pueblo
Bonito. The best
place to find some
kinds of artifacts is
in the garbage
dump of an ancient
civilization. So Judd
and his helpers
went to work and
dug a vertical
trench in a big rub-
bish pile next to

Bill Gillespie studies a sample block of veneer, or facing stones. The veneer helped to support the wall. The stones are all roughly the same size.

the great house. For Judd's purpose, fragments of broken pots,
known as potsherds, were just as good as whole pots. To his sur-
prise, he found examples of the oldest pottery in the top layer
instead of at the bottom of the heap. He dug another trench and
found the same thing. How could that be?

Four years passed before the mystery was solved. It turned out
that long after Pueblo Bonito was well established, the Chacoans
had decided to build another kiva in front of the pueblo. It was to
be a big, round, underground room more than 50 feet across,
which meant moving part of the town dump. In doing this, the
long-ago workers turned over the layers of rubbish. The newest
pots ended up in the bottom layer and the oldest pots on top.

In addition to gaining information from potsherds, Judd discovered that the history of Pueblo Bonito was recorded in the
walls themselves. It was obvious that the great house was the
result of several planned building phases. The Chacoans changed
the pattern of the facing stones over the years, so Judd could tell
which parts of the building were oldest, which came next, and so
on up to those that were the last to be built. But how old was each

text continues on page 18

Building a Great House

The typical ground plan of a great house is in the shape of the letter D. The straight side is a long block of rooms three or four rooms deep. More rooms form the short arms at the top and bottom of the D. The curved side is a single row of rooms that may or may not be connected by doorways. The courtyard area enclosed by the D is dotted with large, circular kivas. Pueblo Bonito has a different ground plan. The view from the top of the nearby mesa shows that the curved side contains the blocks of connected rooms, while the straight side consists of a single line of rooms.

The dense cluster of rooms and kivas on the east side of Pueblo Bonito was built late in the occupation of the pueblo.

Great house walls are made of chunks of sandstone held together by mud mortar. The rough wall is faced on both sides with a layer, or veneer, of carefully cut stones that form a distinctive pattern. This type of construction is called "core and veneer." The pattern of the veneer changed over the years, which helps archaeologists date the building phases.

The earliest veneer is made up of thin, equal-sized pieces of sandstone pressed into the mud mortar spread over the core stones. Later walls are faced with bigger stones, with chips of stone, called spalls, between. Sometimes bands of big stones are separated by layers of small stones. The overall effect is beautiful, although back when people lived in the houses a surface coat of mud plaster hid the pattern. The walls were built from local stone quarried from nearby cliffs. Light-tan sandstone that breaks into chunky blocks is found lower on the cliffs. The dark brown rock at the top is harder and splits at right angles. The builders used this stone to make the intricate patterns of the veneer.

Log beams called vigas (from the Spanish word for beam) supported the roofs. Smaller poles called latillas (from the Spanish word *lata*, for lath, a thin strip of wood) were laid across the beams at right angles. This took an amazing number of trees—200,000—all cut with stone axes. The nearest forests were 20 to 50 miles from the canyon. With no wheeled vehicles, the Chacoans had to carry all these trees by hand, because there were no horses in the Southwest at this time. The logs were probably cut to the required length in the forest and then left to dry for a season before bringing them back to the building site. The entire project points to workers who were well organized with master builders in charge of each stage.

continued from page 15

part? Judd figured that the roof beams would give clues to the exact age of different rooms—if there was just a way to find out when the trees for the beams had been cut.

Pueblo Bonito once stood four stories high and, according to Judd's estimate, contained 800 rooms. (The more accurate estimate today is 600 to 700 rooms and 40 kivas.) He could tell that its massive size was not due to simply adding more and more rooms to an existing building. From the beginning, the designers had planned that the pueblo would be several stories high. The thick-walled rooms on the ground floor form a stable base for the upper stories, which have thinner, lighter walls. This design has stood the test of time.

While moving thousands of tons of earth and stone and blown sand, Judd and his workers took great pains to preserve the building. They strengthened and patched broken walls and replaced door lintels, the short beams across the tops of the doorways. Judd wanted the empty rooms to be able to tell their own story to future generations.

Judd and Wetherill spent many hours thinking about the ancient people who had once lived in the canyon. Wetherill's conclusions had been based mostly on the artifacts he had found and the building itself, but he had no way of knowing exactly when Pueblo Bonito had been inhabited. Judd was eventually able to date some of the rooms, but he, like Wetherill, was looking at discoveries in just one place. The clues to the lost civilization in Chaco Canyon are not all hidden in the great houses. Some clues are in the small houses on the other side of the canyon. Other clues can be found on the valley floor. Some lie in features of the land above the canyon walls.

2

Clues in the Floors, Walls, and Rafters

eil Judd and his crew had just finished excavating a small inner room on the west side of Pueblo Bonito. Before moving on to his next task, Judd knelt down and swept his hand trowel across the dirt floor one last time—and saw the glint of turquoise beads! With rising excitement, he set aside the trowel and picked up an awl and a brush. Working carefully, he used the sharp point of the awl to break up the dirt and the brush to gently clear it away. A short time later, he was staring at an exquisite turquoise necklace and two pairs of earrings. The way the necklace lay coiled and covered with mud and ashes made him think that it had been purposely hidden. "I cannot adequately describe the thrill of that discovery," he wrote later. "A

As ancient Chacoans came into the Casa Rinconada great kiva through its south entry, they saw a central firepit and the north entry opposite. They then took their seats on the stone bench along the wall to watch nighttime ceremonies.

Chacoan peoples used special stones to make many kinds of tools. Some stones, such as chert, were used for saws (top) or knives. Others, such as chalcedony, were crafted into drills of different sizes (middle and bottom) for making holes in beads and pendants.

scrape of the trowel across the ash-strewn floor, a stroke as mechanical as a thousand other strokes made every day, exposed the long-hidden treasure."

The thread that held the beads together had rotted away long ago. Judd had no needle fine enough to go through the small holes in the beads, so he borrowed a banjo string from one of his workers and carefully threaded the beads onto it in the right order. The necklace contained 2,500 beads in four strands.

Large amounts of turquoise have been discovered in Chaco Canyon, although it does not occur there naturally. The turquoise for the jewelry probably came from a mine in the hills about 100 miles east of Chaco. It was turned into ornaments and beads in workshops in the great houses. The Chacoans made the beads by drilling holes in small, roughly shaped disks of turquoise. Archaeologists have found grooved sandstone abraders that were used to round and smooth the strings of beads. The finished necklaces and ornaments served as important items in trade.

While some Chacoans put their energy into making tiny turquoise beads, others were occupied with shaping stones for new great houses. Just half a mile east of Pueblo Bonito, the dramatic ruins of Chetro Ketl nestle against a cliff. Edgar Hewett—the president of New Mexico Normal University—began a study of Chetro Ketl in 1920. He calculated that the massive walls contained 50 million stones, all of which had had to be cut and shaped.

The great houses provided enough mystery and unanswered questions to keep archaeologists busy, but Hewett was also a professor. He needed projects for his students that they could complete in one or two summers. He found them on the south side of the canyon where the ruins of a number of small houses were concealed under mounds of dirt. Some had only eight or 10 rooms; others had up to 30. Most included modest kivas.

The small houses appeared to have been built much earlier than Pueblo Bonito. They were mostly single-story buildings with thin walls made from slabs of rock held together by mud mortar instead of the wide core-and-veneer style found in the great houses. This led archaeologists to speculate that the early Chacoans lived in small-house communities and then built the great houses across the canyon. In the 1930s, Florence Hawley, one of Hewett's students, came up with evidence that contradicted this theory.

After taking a class in dendrochronology—the science of dating wood by tree rings—from A. E. Douglass at the University of Arizona, Hawley applied this method of dating wood to the beams in Chetro Ketl. However, she soon ran into a problem: the beams in the room she was interested in were not all the same age. They were not even close. This turned out to be because the Chacoans often recycled beams from earlier building projects or replaced damaged beams with new wood after a building was completed.

Hawley decided to take wood samples from a large number of beams in each room and examined every sample with a magnifying glass. It was painstaking work, but it eventually paid off. She earned her Ph.D. degree by solving the mystery of when Chetro Ketl was built. The earliest wood in Chetro Ketl was from trees that were cut around A.D. 1000. From 1030 to 1090 was a time of rapid growth and remodeling, but then work slowed down and finally stopped around 1116.

Hawley next investigated the small houses on the south side of the canyon. Pottery artifacts provided the first clue that these houses were built at about the same time as the great houses, not in an earlier period. Dating the beams was complicated by the fact that new houses had been built on top of the remains of older houses. But Hawley was able to prove that the houses were occupied until at least 1088. Clyde Kluckhohn, a co-worker of Hawley's, suggested that two groups of Puebloan Indians with different cultural traditions were living in the canyon at the same time during the 11th century. They probably came there from different

Archaeologists excavate the site of a small house on the south side of Chaco Canyon. Chacoans lived in these small buildings at the same time that other Chacoans occupied great houses such as Pueblo Bonito.

Navajo men assist archaeologists in excavating a small house in Chaco Canyon. Small-house rooms were less than half the size of great-house rooms such as those in Pueblo Bonito.

regions. They may not have spoken the same language. Answers sometimes give rise to more questions.

Casa Rinconada, which sits on a low rise within a few hundred yards of a small-house community, raises still more questions. Because of its architecture and size, it is classified as a "great kiva." Almost all the other great kivas in Chaco Canyon are associated with great houses. Casa Rinconada is some distance from Pueblo Bonito and Chetro Ketl, which lie directly across the canyon, and may have been connected to them. Professor Hewett gave the task of excavating this great kiva to another student, Gordon Vivian. While sifting through the tons of dirt in the summers of 1931 and 1932, Vivian did not know that he—like Richard Wetherill before him—would come to live in Chaco Canyon with his wife and children in a stone-walled hogan, the traditional Navajo style of house, close to Casa Rinconada. Vivian's son Gwinn later followed in his father's footsteps and also became an archaeologist.

Although the excavation of kiva Casa Rinconada turned up very few artifacts—only 385 decorated potsherds—seeing the walls emerge from the dirt of centuries was a reward in itself. The kiva's size and symmetry are awe inspiring. It measures more than 60 feet across. A stone bench runs all the way around the inner wall with evenly spaced niches above it. Gordon Vivian discovered huge sandstone disks that supported the roof beams. Another feature was two square tank-like structures that were probably covered with wood to form foot drums.

Like other kivas, this was an underground ceremonial chamber. It is entered through antechambers, one to the north, another to the south. An underground stone-lined passage leads from the north antechamber to the middle of the floor. It is not hard to picture the leader of a ceremony using this passage to make his dramatic entrance into the dimly lit kiva while the air vibrates with sound as dancers perform on the foot drums.

Gordon and Myrtle Vivian with their young son Gwinn at their stone hogan in Chaco Canyon. This photo was taken in 1936.

Many kivas have a covered hole in the floor called a *sipapu*. The *sipapu* is a symbol of the Puebloan peoples' belief in their unity with the natural world. It is a reminder of their legend that their first people emerged from the underworld. The Hopi people today believe in a Sacred Space that is defined by the seasonal changes of the sun's position on the horizon and by the directions "above" and "below." The orientation of many of the buildings in Chaco Canyon seems to indicate that the ancient people also believed in the importance of place. Many are aligned with particular phases of the sun or moon.

It is very probable that in times of drought the Chacoans gathered together to ask the clouds to release their life-giving rain or

text continues on page 26

Closing the Gap in the Tree-Ring Diary

Andrew Ellicott Douglass was an astronomer, but he spent more time looking at trees than at the stars. He wanted to find out if sunspots—dark spots that occur on the sun—affected the weather here on earth. Sunspots vary in a roughly 11-year cycle. Douglass knew that trees put on more growth in wet years than in dry ones, so the rings from wet years are wider. He also knew that the growth rings of pine trees in the Southwest provide a very accurate picture of the cycle of wet and dry years. He hoped to show that the weather records hidden in tree rings would match up with the cycle of sunspot activity. In his quest for astronomical answers, Douglass founded the science of dendrochronology.

Douglass used a cylindrical boring tool called a wood corer to cut across the growth rings from the bark to the center of the trunk. He started out recording the sequence of the rings in living trees. He then obtained samples of old pine logs from a lumberyard. The pattern of rings in the older wood overlapped with the inner rings in the living trees. This enabled him to take his weather diary farther back through time. The next step was to find even earlier wood in the beams of old buildings. He eventually developed a master chronology—a diary of wet years and dry years—that went all the way back to 1380.

Douglass soon realized that his weather diary could be of great help to archaeologists. He obtained samples of wood from sites such as Pueblo Bonito and Cliff Palace in Mesa Verde and put together a tree-ring diary for prehistoric times. But he could not use his new diary to date Pueblo Bonito, because there was a gap between his ancient records and 1380. Then, in June 1929, he made an exciting discovery. In a ruin, he found an old wooden beam that bridged the gap. He had solved the mystery of the age of the great houses in Chaco Canyon. The beam completed a tree-ring diary or master chronology that now goes from the present day all the way back to 322 B.C.

Archaeologists match the width of the annual growth rings of trees to determine the age of wood found on a survey site. The growth rings of core sample A when matched with core samples B and C create a "calendar" that reveals the moisture level, and subsequent tree growth, from 2000 to 1850.

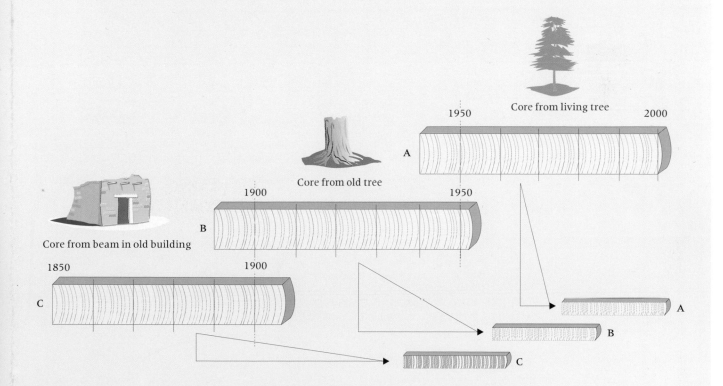

Core from living tree

1950   2000

A

Core from old tree

1900   1950

B

Core from beam in old building

1850   1900

C

A

B

C

continued from page 23

Images of the hump-backed flute player Kokopelli, a sacred figure who appears as a priest, trickster, and magician in Native American mythology, were found carved into Chaco Canyon's upper terraces.

snow, as Puebloans do to this day. The vast space enclosed by the walls of Casa Rinconada seems to faintly echo the chant of the people of the San Ildefonso Pueblo, 100 miles west of Chaco:

Hasten clouds from the four quarters:
Come snow in plenty, that water
May be abundant when summer comes;
Come ice, cover the fields, that the planting may yield in
    abundance,
Let all hearts be glad.

3

The Population Puzzle

Chaco Canyon has its own wild beauty, but in many ways it is a surprising place for the rise of a successful civilization. The average rainfall is less than nine inches a year. In the summer, temperatures often reach more than 100 degrees Fahrenheit and in winter they can fall to as low as zero degrees. Spring gales carry off the thin layer of sandy soil in swirling dust storms. In spite of these difficult conditions, the

Young Hopi women used manos (handheld stones) and metates (the concave stones on the ground) to grind corn in the early 1900s. Chacoan women used similar stone tools to prepare cornmeal.

Through inventive engineering, the Chacoans were able to collect and route enough rainwater to sustain fertile crops.

ancient people managed to grow enough corn, beans, and squash to feed themselves and their families. Their agricultural tools were simple—a digging stick for planting, and a hoe or spade made by lashing a flat stone to a forked stick. Once the corn was harvested, it was ground into meal in a shallow stone basin called a metate using a mano, or grinding stone. The Chacoans also ate wild plants and supplemented their diet with meat from turkeys they raised. They hunted rabbits and deer with bows and arrows.

The annual growth rings in the area's trees show that the weather pattern was much the same 1,000 years ago as it is today. About half of the annual rainfall occurs in July and August. While Gordon Vivian and his family were living in Chaco Canyon, they had plenty of opportunity to observe the summer rains. All through June, Gwinn and his two sisters, Ann and Ruth, ran barefoot under the hot sun. In July, the weather was less predictable. By late afternoon, billowing white clouds would boil up and then turn dark as crackling lightning announced a coming storm. When the first drops fell the children ran for cover. The rain came down in such torrents that it even drowned out the rumbling thunder.

The typical summer cloudburst would stop as suddenly as it had begun, but for some time afterward water would pour off the mesa and cascade down the small side canyons, or rincons. Because the Chacoans were skilled builders, Gordon Vivian was sure that they must have had some way of collecting and distributing this water. He soon found evidence of an efficient irrigation system. Later, Gwinn expanded on his father's work.

The Chacoan irrigation system depended on dams and canals. After a rainstorm a dam at the mouth of each side canyon collected the water that fell from the cliff top. The water was then channeled into a stone-lined canal, which emptied into a head gate with narrow openings that could be blocked or left open to control the water's flow into ditches. The ditches led to large plots of many individual gardens.

In the summer of 1967, Gwinn Vivian excavated a dam that had been built across one of the main side canyons. It was a massive structure more than 120 feet long and 7 feet high. The water emptied into a canal through a gate near the middle of the dam. The long, curving, masonry-lined canal directed the water to 24 acres of bordered gardens that were laid out in neat rectangles. Gwinn Vivian calculated that a summer thunderstorm that produced 1 1/4 inches of rain in an hour would have provided the Peñasco Blanco gardens with 540,000 gallons of water—half a gallon per square foot. The Chacoan genius for building and engineering allowed a large number of people to live in that otherwise dry and rugged canyon.

One question has intrigued archaeologists over the years: Exactly how big was the population in the canyon when the culture was at its height? In the 1970s, John Corbett decided that it was time to find an answer. Corbett had attended Hewett's summer field schools back in the 1930s. He was now the chief archaeologist for the National Park Service, so he was in a position

Water flows from a canal into a small ditch after a rainstorm in Chaco Canyon. In prehistoric times, the ditch carried the water to fields of corn, squash, and beans.

In what became known as Atlatl Cave, an archaeologist found food remains and a broken atlatl, evidence of very early human occupation in Chaco Canyon.

to organize what became known as the Chaco Project. A team of archaeologists would try to answer the population question, and almost every other question that had been asked about Chaco Canyon.

The project got under way in 1971 with four archaeologists surveying the canyon. Unlike the early archaeologists, they did not arm themselves with shovels. They simply walked over long strips of land across the mesa and down through the canyon, recording every prehistoric site and artifact they found.

The following year, 12 archaeologists led by Alden Hayes, another of Hewett's former students, took part in the survey. They identified chips of stone where an ancient hunter had stopped to fashion an arrow point. They discovered hearths, baking pits, and crumbled walls. They recorded rock art on the cliffs. They found evidence that the Basket Makers had lived on the mesa in pithouse villages as long ago as A.D. 500.

A pithouse was an underground or partly underground room. Smoke from the central firepit escaped through a hole in the middle of the flat, mud-and-wood roof. This same hole served as the doorway, reached from inside by a ladder. Around the middle of the eighth century, people moved down into the canyon.

The round pithouses evolved into kivas, and small pueblos were created by grouping three or four houses together. The earliest pueblos were built with poles and adobe, but this soon gave way to building with stone. Most of the great houses were constructed at the height of Chaco civilization in the late 900s and early 1000s.

The survey was just a beginning. The team went on to study many different achievements of the ancient people—irrigation systems, roads, stairways, and the Chaco influence outside the canyon. New tools, such as aerial and infrared photography, enabled the archaeologists to gather information without taking buildings apart. They did do some excavating, but the approach to digging up the past was changing. They no longer removed the entire blanket of sand and soil that the winds had deposited over the centuries. For example, when they studied Pueblo Alto, a great house on the top of the mesa, they excavated only 7 percent of the rooms.

One reason for no longer doing extensive digging is that the covering of dry sandy soil is a good preservative. Walls that were excavated by Wetherill and Judd are showing signs of weather damage. Some ruins have been reburied to preserve them. Another reason for doing less digging is out of respect for the present-day descendants of the ancient people.

Improvements made to traditional tools also allowed the Chaco Project archaeologists to come up with better results. By the 1970s, wood corers had a much finer bore than those used by Florence Hawley. They left a smaller hole in the beam, and better microscopes were available to make reading the pattern easier. Using a fine-bore corer, archaeologist Thomas Windes dated wood samples from the small roof latillas instead of the large viga main beams. They provided more accurate records, because the latillas were not recycled or replaced the way the big beams often were.

In the early 1980s, Alden Hayes tackled the population question: How many people had lived in the great houses? He based his calculations on the average size of a Chacoan family and the number of rooms a family would occupy. His average family consisted of 4 or 5 people. This figure is the average size of Puebloan

Archaeologists found these small, delicate figures in red ocher (an earthy mineral used as a pigment) on the walls of Atlatl Cave in Chaco Canyon. The human figures in these Archaic Period drawings may represent both men and women. An animal, probably a deer, is painted below their feet.

James Judge, a National Park Service ranger, uses an alidade, an instrument used to determine direction, to make a map of an archaeological site.

families in recent historic times, from 1744 to 1952. It may have been lower 1,000 years ago, due to a higher rate of infant death, but was unlikely to have been higher. Hayes assumed that every family occupied three rooms. He also figured that at any period of time some of the rooms were abandoned or filled with rubbish. Taking all those variables into account, he came up with a peak population of 5,652 people. Most archaeologists agree on the range of 4,500 to 6,000 people.

Thomas Windes took a different approach. He estimated the number of families by counting the firepits in the great houses. He reasoned that a firepit was essential for cooking and heating, especially during the cold winters, so the number of firepits would reflect the number of families. Most of these hearths are found in ground-story rooms. Windes suggested that the upper rooms were left empty or were used for storage. He figured that the maximum population might have been only 2,000 people.

Another clue to the size of long-ago populations is the number of burials in a region. But only a relatively small number of skeletons have been found in Chaco Canyon. No one has discovered a cemetery. Many of the skeletons that have been found were in rooms in Pueblo Bonito. Others were found in the refuse piles at the small-house sites. The practice of providing the dead with turquoise ornaments and pottery to accompany them on their journey to the Underworld may have lured early pothunters to the area, who destroyed the graves before archaeologists had the chance to examine them. The missing skeletons pose yet another mystery. The great houses in Chaco Canyon do not give up their secrets easily.

Pottery Styles

The Chacoans made black-on-white pottery with zigzag designs and closely spaced lines called hatching. They used a mineral paint that gave clear, sharp lines. The paint was made by grinding up red or brown stones that contained iron minerals and mixing the resulting powder with water. Pottery brought in from the Mesa Verde area is also found in Chaco Canyon. Mesa Verde potters used plant-based pigments that resulted in designs with a softer outline. The paint was most commonly made from Rocky Mountain beeweed. The leaves and stems were boiled with water to produce a thick, black paste that was then diluted with a little water to produce the paint.

This large Chacoan jug may have been used in special ceremonies.

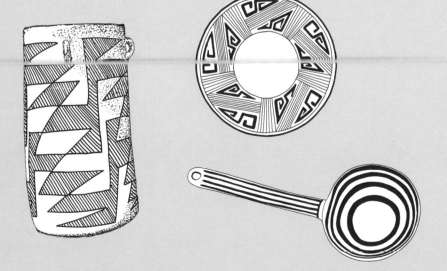

Potters in Chaco Canyon painted their white bowls, jars, and ladles with black designs. These motifs changed over time, and archaeologists can often determine the approximate dates of when people lived at a site by the designs on broken pieces of pottery found there.

4

Mysterious Superhighways

Gwinn Vivian stands on a Chacoan road that he originally thought was a water canal. Low stone walls border both sides of the road.

When Gwinn Vivian was excavating the water system near the great house Pueblo Alto, he began to have serious doubts about the section that he had named "Canal 3." To be part of the system, the water would have had to flow uphill. He finally decided that what he had thought was the bottom of a canal was really part of an ancient roadbed.

The Chacoan roads are another of the great unsolved mysteries of Chaco Canyon. Why did people who had no wheeled vehicles, not even hand-pulled carts, build more than 200 miles of roads? These are not mere walking trails. They are wide roads edged with stones or low ridges of earth and rubble. For mile after mile, they follow an arrow-straight course across the landscape, going over obstacles instead of curving around them. When a road does change direction, it makes a wide-angled turn and then continues in a straight line.

Gwinn Vivian's "uphill canal" revived an interest in roads among some of the archaeologists involved in the Chaco Project. The ancient roads show up better when the landscape is seen from above, so they took a series of aerial photographs using black-and-white, color, and infrared film.

By the end of the summer of 1972, 200 miles of roads had been identified in aerial photographs. The next step took longer. The archaeologists had to verify the roads by what they call "ground truth." Two-person teams walked the length of the roads, taking measurements and still more pictures. Not all of the lines on the aerial photos were ultimately identified as roads, but those that were nearly always measured exactly 30 feet wide. On sloping ground the lower side of the road was often built up. In places where the ground level changed suddenly, ramps made walking smoother. Steps cut into the cliff connected roads on the mesa with the canyon floor below.

The roads all lead to Chaco, but these same roads have led present-day archaeologists outside the canyon to study scattered communities that are known as "outliers." Some of these outliers have been buried by centuries of blowing sand. They are nothing more than bumps on the landscape and can be recognized only by an expert. Others are so similar to the great houses that the Chacoan connection is obvious.

Aztec, which is by far the largest of the outliers, is 15 miles northeast of the present-day city of Farmington. (In spite of its

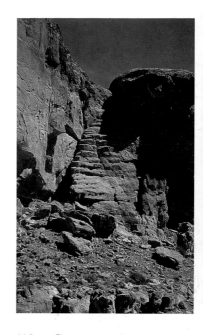

When Chacoan road builders came to the edge of a cliff, they cut wide steps in the sandstone so people using the road could climb down into Chaco Canyon. These steps are located near the Hungo Pavi great house.

Chacoan roads were used to transport jewelry and other precious objects.

name it has nothing to do with the Aztec culture in Mexico.) The main pueblo had more than 400 rooms and was built between A.D. 1110 and 1120. A great kiva stands in the middle of the plaza. About 10 miles south of Aztec is the Salmon Ruin outlier, a medium-sized great house two to three stories high, with about 175 rooms. The roof beams are mostly from trees that were cut between A.D. 1088 and 1090. The pueblo was occupied for only a very short span of time, until around 1116. Archaeologists can tell from pottery fragments that people from Mesa Verde reoccupied the building between 1185 and 1263. By 1285, the great house was again deserted.

In 1980, Gretchen Obenhauf, an anthropology student at the University of New Mexico, used outliers such as the Salmon Ruin as a starting point for finding new roads. She examined photographs, looking for faint dark lines leading away from the outlier toward known roads. The fact that the roads all ran in straight lines made the search easier, but some of the old roads will never be traced, because they have been covered by wind-blown sand or have been lost to erosion or modern activities.

One purpose of the roads was almost certainly to connect the outliers and Chaco Canyon. A well-marked route would make transporting goods over long distances easier, and working together to build the roads would help to unite the scattered communities. Archaeologists have found a great many broken pots along the Great North Road leading to the Salmon Ruin, but that does not mean that the pots themselves were an item of trade. They may have held products like corn and beans that were brought from the fields around the outliers to Chaco for food.

However, there must be reasons other than trade for all those roads that lead to Chaco. Foot traffic does not need a 30-foot-wide highway. In places roads run parallel to one another, rather like a north- and southbound freeway. There are even sections with double parallel roads. Some of the minor roads are 15 feet wide, exactly half the width of the major roads.

Some archaeologists now believe that the roads may have served as ceremonial highways, with different tribes each using their own part of the road. A present-day Hopi Indian has suggested that the roads might have had a symbolic significance. Some of the Pueblo Indian legends recall the migration routes of the ancestral kin groups who came from the north, the south, and the southwest. None came from the east. Is it significant that almost all of the main roads into Chaco also run in only the same three directions? Could the Chacoans have had similar legends?

The big pueblo at Aztec was completed in a very short space of time early in the 12th century. By the middle of the century it was deserted. In Chetro Ketl, the most recent beams are from A.D. 1116. Florence Hawley concluded that all building and remodeling had stopped by 1120. In Pueblo Bonito, there were no new projects after 1130. The great house Wijiji in the eastern part of the canyon was built in the early 1100s, but it may never have been occupied. So much planning and labor . . . and then nothing.

This brings up the question that always comes to mind when people view Pueblo Bonito's towering walls, empty rooms, and silent kivas: What caused such a successful culture to suddenly disappear? The answer is that when we use the words "suddenly" and "disappear," we are asking the wrong question. There is no evidence that the end came suddenly. The Chacoans were not wiped out by warfare or disease. It is true that the great houses were later occupied by other groups, including people from Mesa Verde, but these people moved into already deserted buildings. They did not drive the Chacoans out. And there was no mass migration from

Two archaeologists dig to expose a sandstone wall that bordered a part of a Chacoan road. This road went from Pueblo Alto into Chaco Canyon, which is visible in the background.

Ancient Chacoans left this record of flute players (top), a blanket design (bottom right), a woman giving birth (center right), and mountain sheep (bottom). Anasazi stone-carved rock art may tell stories of migrations, hunting, and ceremonies.

the canyon. There seems to have been a gradual recognition that it was time to move on. Over quite a period of time, families and extended family groups simply packed up their belongings and left the region. Some may have joined up with other groups who had left earlier. Others may have been accepted into established villages. These many possiblities make them difficult to trace.

Tree-ring diaries for the Chaco region explain the timing of the move. The years between A.D. 1090 and 1100 were unusually dry. Even during good years, the farmers in the canyon had a hard time producing enough food for the growing population. The dry years forced people to go outside the canyon. Then the rain returned, and with it came a flurry of building early in the 12th century. But the wet weather lasted for only a generation or so. The year 1130 was dry, and this time drought persisted for 50 years. In a way, its very success led to the civilization's collapse. The land could no longer support so many people.

The culture of the Chacoan people is defined by the great houses that they built in the canyon. When they moved out of the area they could not take their houses with them nor their complex irrigation systems and roads. Because they left in small groups over a period of time, they did not rebuild the huge pueblos. There was no need to do so. They were moving on to a new life. What they did take with them was their wisdom, their skills, their legends, and their ceremonies. They still made pottery and fashioned jewelry from turquoise. They told their children the old legends and they built new kivas.

This is why archaeologists today no longer rely only on shovels when they are digging up the past. Instead, they go out among present-day Pueblo Indians and listen to their stories. These provide a link with the past, but as they listen, they realize that they will never solve all the mysteries. Nine hundred years is a long, long time, especially when there are no written records. Very few people can trace their ancestors back through 36 generations.

Even on the brightest day, a slight air of melancholy seems to cling to the ruined walls of Pueblo Bonito. Visitors to the canyon cannot help feeling a little sad when they see the faint outline of gardens that were once green with beans and corn, and the dark imprint of the straight roads across the mesa. But at the same time, the great houses are a splendid reminder of what people with a vision who work together in harmony can accomplish.

Mollie Toll collects samples of earth that contain microscopic pollen grains. The scientific study of pollen is useful for telling what kinds of food Chacoan people ate and how plants adjusted to changes in the climate.

Sun Daggers and Bright Stars

A shaft of sunlight shines straight across a spiral cut into a sandstone cliff on Fajada Butte in Chaco Canyon. Anna Sofaer, an artist and filmmaker, discovered this "Sun Dagger" near the time of the summer solstice and realized the ancient Chacoans had created a special place to mark this event every year.

Ancient people from many different areas and cultures were familiar with the movement of the sun, stars, and moon, and the rhythm of the changing seasons. Artist Anna Sofaer has found evidence that the Chacoans were no exception. In mid-June 1977 she was climbing Fajada Butte, a huge table rock near the middle of the canyon, when she discovered a petroglyph.

It was not, in itself, an exciting find—a coiled spiral about the size of a dinner plate. It was also hard to see. It was almost hidden by three slabs of stone that rested against the cliff. What was exciting was that the sun's rays shining between the slabs formed a dagger of light that fell across the spiral.

Sofaer returned on June 22 and found—as she had predicted—that the dagger of light pierced the center of the spiral. The sun dagger marked the longest day of the year, known as the summer solstice. In fact, it did not just mark the day, it showed the precise

Did the ancient Chacoans record the explosion of a star (a supernova) in A.D. 1054? Some archaeologists and astronomers believe this pictograph near the Peñasco Blanco great house was painted to mark that event.

moment when the sun was at its highest point in the sky. From that moment, the days begin to grow shorter each year.

Near Peñasco Blanco, a pictograph of an outstretched hand, a crescent moon, and a big star has caused a lot of speculation among astronomers. Back in A.D. 1054, a new bright light, about five times as bright as the planet Venus, suddenly appeared in the sky. Because of its position in the sky it is called the Crab Nebula supernova. Did some Chacoan stargazer record this event on the rock near Peñasco Blanco? The Chacoans who were living in the canyon at the time would certainly have noticed this new bright star. Computer models show that near sunrise on the morning of July 4, 1054, the supernova was located in the sky two degrees from the waning moon, just as it appears in the pictograph.

An Interview with R. Gwinn Vivian

by Margaret Anderson

The first home that Gwinn Vivian can remember is a hogan near Casa Rinconada in Chaco Canyon. He had two younger sisters, named Ann and Ruth. His father, Gordon Vivian, was an archaeologist with the University of New Mexico. The Vivian family lived in the canyon from 1936 until 1941.

Margaret Anderson Spending your early years in Chaco Canyon must have influenced your choice of career. How old were you when you first knew you wanted to be an archaeologist?

Gwinn Vivian I remember being swept up by the idea of doing archaeology when I was 11. We had just returned to the canyon after the Second World War and I spent the whole morning digging in the Pueblo Bonito refuse mound. I found a lot of potsherds, which I presented to my father at lunch. Though Mother claimed that I decided on my career long before that. When I was three, I found a mano—a milling stone—and I gave it to her, saying, "Keep this for me until I become an archaeologist!"

MA Chaco Canyon is very remote. Where did you and your sisters go to school?

GV At first we were taught at home, but when we were older we stayed in Albuquerque with Mother during the school year, while Dad worked at Chaco. We went back to Chaco every vacation and any time Dad needed help. Once he called to say that he had found a mass of carved and painted wood crushed under a collapsed roof and wall in Chetro Ketl.

Gwinn Vivian and Margaret Anderson on a recent visit to Chaco Canyon (top). A young Gwinn Vivian during a backbreaking excavation of a ruin in Chaco Canyon (bottom).

We jumped into our old blue Plymouth sedan and headed to the canyon. We spent the next week uncovering hundreds of fragments of exquisitely painted birds and other figures. One morning while I was excavating my way backward across the room I suddenly dropped into the room below; it was a drop of only about four feet, because the room below was partly filled with soil. Before Dad hauled me out, he wanted to know everything about the room—and I would swear that Mother made some teasing remark about it probably being a good place to leave me!

MA Were you paid for working?

GV When I was around 12, I earned 10 cents an hour for washing potsherds. I spent it all on Tarzan books. They cost $1.98 each in the Montgomery Ward catalog. When a new book arrived, I'd read all day. Then it was back to sherd-washing again!

MA What jobs did you have when you were older?

GV In the summer of 1951, I worked on a crew that was putting in a new road up the canyon. On weekends, Dad and I started a survey of the Chacra Mesa to the east of Chaco. I used the results of the survey in my thesis at the University of New Mexico.

MA You seem to have worked very closely with your father.

GV Yes, I did. In the late 1950s he became very interested in Chacoan water control and I had the opportunity to help him. When his early death in 1966 left much of this work unfinished, I determined to carry it forward. I spent the summer of 1967 and a full year in 1970–71 doing all the things Dad had taught me—surveying,

test excavating, note taking, photography—and thinking about what I had found.

MA What was your most important discovery?

GV I don't know about my most important discovery, but my most memorable one happened in 1967. I was working at Pueblo Alto on the cliff above Pueblo Bonito with Greg Staley, a high school student helper. One day we took a side trip down the mesa. At the bottom of a small wash we came across a prehistoric bowl lying there out in the open. We stared at it, not sure what to do. I finally decided to dig a small hole in the side of the bank and rebury it. While I was scraping away the dirt, I saw the side of another bowl. We got out our trowels and partially excavated this bowl, but before we were finished another bowl had appeared. And then another, and another!

By early evening we had cleared about a dozen bowls and they were still continuing back into the soil. We went back to camp, wondering what we ought to do.

Early the next morning Greg and I went back and covered them all up, including the bowl that had been lying in the bottom of the wash. I memorized the spot and marked it with a piece of greasewood.

The next year I walked down that wash and went to the spot where I was sure we had found the pots, but it did not look exactly right. So I walked further down the wash, saw another spot—but no, it was wrong, too!

I have since been back to that place and have had the same experience every time. So there it is: a great discovery waiting to be rediscovered!

Glossary

adobe Claylike soil used in the American Southwest for plastering walls and making building blocks.

Anasazi The Navajo name given to a prehistoric group of American Indians who lived in the plateau region of northern Arizona and New Mexico, and southern Utah and Colorado. Many American Indians prefer the term "Ancestral Puebloan."

awl A pointed wood, bone, or metal hand tool used by Native Americans for making holes in leather, baskets, cloth, and wood.

Basket Makers An early American Indian group (around A.D. 500) named for their skill in basket making.

dendrochronology The science of dating wood by examining patterns of tree-ring growth.

excavate To remove soil and sand from newly discovered buildings and artifacts when looking for archaeological data.

foot drum Rectangular pit found in the floors of kivas. The pits were covered with boards and when danced on would produce a deep, drumlike sound.

great house A planned and specialized form of pueblo built by Chacoan peoples from about A.D. 850–A.D. 1150.

hogan A circular Navajo Indian dwelling with walls of logs or stone and a log roof covered by soil.

infrared A kind of photography used by archaeologists that records light wavelengths. Manmade and natural features show up in different colors, which helps to differentiate them on the ground.

interpretations The ways archaeologists use information collected from surveys and excavations to reconstruct what may have happened in the past.

kiva A circular or square ceremonial building, mostly built underground, that is used by Puebloan Indians.

latillas Small poles laid across roof beams (vigas) to form the ceiling of a pueblo house.

mano A handheld grinding stone that is used with a stone basin (metate).

mesa The Spanish word for "table" given to flat-topped mountains in the Southwest.

metate A stone basin for grinding corn.

outlier A building or group of buildings that look like Chaco great houses but are found as far as 100 miles from Chaco Canyon.

petroglyph A drawing that is carved or scratched into rock.

pictograph A drawing that is painted on rock.

pithouse An early underground dwelling.

potsherds (or sherds) Broken fragments of pottery.

pueblo A many-roomed building in the Southwestern United States that houses several families.

rincon A small side canyon.

sipapu A small hole found in the floor of a kiva where spirit ancestors emerge from an earlier underground world.

survey The process used by archaeologists to record the location of past human activities, such as house building, farming, and hunting.

vigas Large roof beams in a pueblo house.

Further Reading

The Archaeology of the Southwest

Douglass, Andrew Ellicott. "The Secret of the Southwest Solved by Talkative Tree Rings." *National Geographic*, Dec. 1929, 737–70.

Goodman, Susan E. *Stones, Bones, and Petroglyphs: Digging into Southwest Archaeology.* New York: Atheneum, 1998.

Judd, Neil Merton. "Everyday Life in Pueblo Bonito." *National Geographic*, Sept. 1925, 227–62.

Lister, Robert H., and Florence C. Lister. *Those Who Came Before— Southwestern Archaeology in the National Park System.* Tucson: Southwest Parks and Monuments Association, 1993.

Petersen, David. *Chaco Culture National Historical Park.* Chicago: Children's Press, 1999.

Native Americans of the Southwest

Arnold, Caroline. *The Ancient Cliff Dwellers of Mesa Verde.* New York: Clarion, 1992.

Noble, David Grant. *101 Questions About Ancient Indians of the Southwest.* Tucson: Southwest Parks and Monuments Association, 1998.

Powell, Susanne. *The Pueblos.* New York: Franklin Watts, 1993.

Sears, Bryan P., and G. S. Prentzas. *The Hopi Indians.* New York: Chelsea House, 1994.

Sneve, Virginia Driving Hawk. *The Navajos.* New York: Holiday House, 1993.

Yue, Charlotte, and David Yue. *The Pueblo.* Boston: Houghton Mifflin, 1990.

Chaco Canyon and Related Sites

Chacoan culture is known best from a group of archaeological sites in Chaco Canyon located near the center of a large region called the San Juan Basin in northwestern New Mexico. Many other archaeological sites with cultural connections to Chaco Canyon are found in the basin. For almost 100 years the National Park Service and other federal, state, and tribal agencies have worked hard to protect some of the most important of these sites.

GOING TO CHACO CULTURE NATIONAL HISTORICAL PARK

P.O. Box 220
Nageezi, NM 87037-0220
505-786-7014
www.nps.gov/chcu

Chaco Culture National Historical Park is managed by the National Park Service and is open to the public year-round. There is a museum of Chacoan culture at the Visitor Center as well as ranger-guided and self-guided tours of the major ruins. The campground is open year-round; however there are no lodging, gasoline, repair services, or food at the park.

AZTEC RUINS NATIONAL MONUMENT

Aztec, New Mexico,
50 miles north of Chaco Canyon
A National Park Service museum and guided tours of a Chacoan great house help trace Chacoan culture in the early 1100s, when some ancient people were leaving Chaco Canyon and moving to places like the Aztec Ruins.

CHIMNEY ROCK RUIN

95 miles northeast of Chaco Canyon
The San Juan National Forest protects this late Chacoan outlier and provides information on the ancient people living here in the late 1000s and early 1100s.

LOWRY RUIN

120 miles northwest of Chaco Canyon near Cortez, Colorado
This late Chacoan outlier great house is protected by the Colorado Bureau of Land Management. Information about Lowry Ruin is available at the site.

MESA VERDE NATIONAL PARK

85 miles northwest of Chaco Canyon near Mancos, Colorado
A large museum and guided tours of archaeological sites, many with connections to Chacoan culture. People from Mesa Verde may have built some late sites in Chaco Canyon.

SALMON RUIN

Bloomfield, New Mexico, 45 miles north of Chaco Canyon
The San Juan County Archaeological Society has preserved this late Chacoan outlier and relates the site to Chaco Canyon through museum exhibits and tours of the great house.

WHITE HOUSE, CANYON DE CHELLY NATIONAL MONUMENT

85 miles west of Chaco Canyon near Chinle, Arizona
Descriptive panels at the site and pamphlet information at the National Park Service Museum describe this late Chacoan outlier great house. To visit the site you must walk 2.5 miles (round trip) into and out of the canyon.

VILLAGE OF THE GREAT KIVAS

75 miles southwest of Chaco Canyon on the Zuni Indian Reservation
The Zuni tribe protects this Chacoan outlier great house. The site may be closed to the public; contact the Ashawi Awan Museum at 505-782-4403.

Index

R. Gwinn Vivian is a former curator of archaeology at the Arizona State Museum, University of Arizona. He spent his childhood in Chaco Canyon, where his father was an archaeologist with the National Park Service. He continues to conduct research in the Chaco region. He received the New Mexico Heritage Preservation Award for his book *The Chacoan Prehistory of the San Juan Basin* and recently co-authored *The Chaco Handbook.*

Margaret Anderson has written more than 20 books, both fiction and nonfiction, for young readers. Her books have received such honors as a *Smithsonian Magazine* Notable Book listing, Children's Books of Distinction Award from *Riverbank Review,* and a National Science Teachers Association Award for Outstanding Trade Science Book for Children. She lives near Corvallis, Oregon.

Brian Fagan is professor of anthropology at the University of California, Santa Barbara. He is internationally known for his books on archaeology, among them *The Adventure of Archaeology, The Rape of the Nile,* and the *Oxford Companion to Archaeology.*

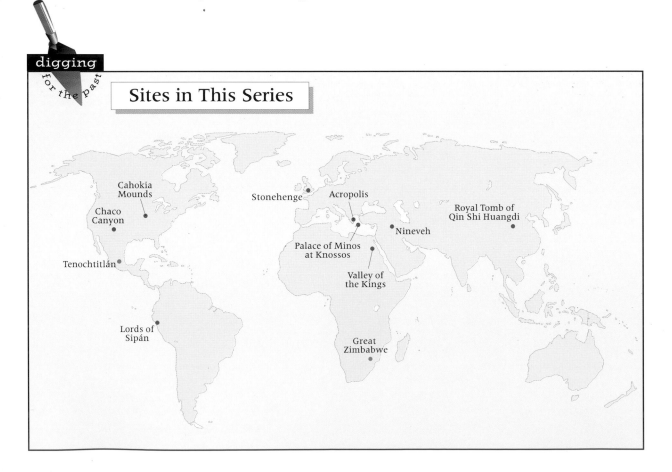

digging
for the past

Sites in This Series

Cahokia Mounds

Chaco Canyon

Stonehenge

Acropolis

Royal Tomb of Qin Shi Huangdi

Nineveh

Palace of Minos at Knossos

Tenochtitlán

Valley of the Kings

Lords of Sipán

Great Zimbabwe